Dragon Training

Tony Bradman • Jon Stuart

D1465377

Contents

OXFORD
UNIVERSITY PRESS

Macro Marvel
(billionaire inventor)

Welcome to Micro World!

Macro Marvel invented Micro World – a micro-sized theme park where you have to shrink to get in.

A computer called *CODE* controls Micro World and all the robots inside – MITEs and BITEs.

A MITE

A BITE

Disaster strikes!

CODE goes wrong on opening day.
CODE wants to shrink the world.

Macro Marvel is trapped inside the park …

Enter Team X!

Four micro agents – *Max, Cat, Ant* and *Tiger* – are sent to rescue Macro Marvel and defeat CODE.

Mini Marvel joins Team X.

Mini Marvel
(Macro's daughter)

In the last book ...

* Mini read about the Dragon-BITE on her Gizmo.

* The BITE shot fire at Max, Ant and Mini.

* Max used his force shield.

* They escaped.

**CODE key
(2 collected)**

You are in the
Dragon Quest zone.

3

Before you read

Sound checker
Say the sounds.

oy   **ou**

Sound spotter
Blend the sounds.

| a | nn | oy |

| m | ou | th |

| a | b | ou | t |

| t | r | ai | n | i | ng |

Tricky words
do
come

Into the zone

Do you think a dragon would make a good pet?

Can You Train a Dragon?

"This book is about training dragons," said Tiger.

Dragons' Dens

Do not go down into a dragon's den. This will annoy the dragon.

Looking After Dragons

A dragon needs lots of sleep.

It needs a drink.

Training Pet Dragons

1 Sing sweetly.
Dragons like the sound!

2 Let the dragon come to you.

3 Pat the dragon often. Do not go near a dragon's mouth! It is boiling hot!

Sitting on a Dragon

4 If you train the dragon well, it might let you sit on its back. Enjoy the flight!

Now you have read ...
Can You Train a Dragon?

Text checker

How do you train a dragon?

	👍	👎
• Go into the dragon's den.	Yes	No
• Sing to the dragon.	Yes	No
• Pat the dragon.	Yes	No

MITE fun

Would you like to fly on a dragon's back?

> Can you remember
> what a dragon needs?

Before you read

Sound checker
Say the sounds.

oy   ou

Sound spotter
Blend the sounds.

b	oy

r	ou	n	d

sh	ou	t	ed

e	n	j	oy	i	ng

Tricky words
come
do
some

Into the zone
What do you think will happen
if Tiger sits on a dragon?

12

Dragon Flight

Come to me, boy.

Tiger was training a green dragon.
He sang sweetly.

"Come on, Tiger," said Cat.
"Let's get the CODE key."
"Not yet," said Tiger.

The dragon crouched down and Tiger got on its back.

The dragon whizzed round and round in the air.

17

"I'm enjoying this," said Tiger.
He made the dragon go up
and down.

Suddenly the dragon shot off quickly.

"Stop! Too fast!" shouted Tiger.

The dragon sped towards
the ground.
"It won't do what I say!"
yelled Tiger.

Then Tiger tugged on the straps.
The dragon slowed down.
It landed softly on the soil.

The dragon had spotted
Cat with some dragon food!

"Thanks, Cat. I'm glad you found us," said Tiger. "Some dragons are not very easy to train!"

Now you have read ...
Dragon Flight

Text checker

How do you fly a dragon? Find the other
half of each instruction.

Sing to the dragon	to slow down.
Tap the dragon on the right	to turn left.
Tap the dragon on the left	to turn right.
Tug the straps	to make it come to you.

MITE fun

Look back at the story. What did Cat and Tiger do ...

... at the beginning?

... in the middle?

... at the end?

OXFORD
UNIVERSITY PRESS

Great Clarendon Street, Oxford, OX2 6DP,
United Kingdom

Oxford University Press is a department of the University of Oxford.
It furthers the University's objective of excellence in research, scholarship,
and education by publishing worldwide. Oxford is a registered trade mark of
Oxford University Press in the UK and in certain other countries

British Library Cataloguing in Publication Data
Data available

978-0-19-834012-6

9 10 8

Paper used in the production of this book is a natural, recyclable product
made from wood grown in sustainable forests. The manufacturing process conforms
to the environmental regulations of the country of origin.

Printed in China by Hing Yip

Acknowledgements
Character illustrations by Jonatronix Ltd, Senior Art Director: Jon Stuart, 3D artist: Sean Frisby
Series editors: Maureen Lewis, Di Hatchett
Phonics consultant: Marilyn Joyce
Teaching notes written by Rachael Sutherland
Project X concept by Rod Theodorou and Emma Lynch

**Team X and Mini still need
to find the CODE key. They're
running out of time …**

Now you need to read
Into the Cave.

Project X

Book Band 4
Blue

Oxford
Level 4

Letters and Sounds
Phases 4 and 5
Focus GPCs: oy (/oi/),
ou (/ou/)
Tricky words: some,
come, do

CODE

11

Team X face their biggest challenge yet ... to battle the BITEs, rescue Macro Marvel and stop CODE!

Can You Train a Dragon?
Tiger and Cat see how to train a dragon.

Dragon Flight
Tiger trains a dragon so well that it lets him sit on its back. Then it swoops up into the air!

KU-007-09

CODE

1

The Web

Alison Hawes
Jon Stuart

OXFORD

In this book

Focus GPCs

- j, v, w, z, zz

Tricky words

- they, he, are, she

Team X words

- Max, Tiger, Mini, BITE, Team X, CODE key

See *Project X CODE* Teaching and Assessment Handbook 1 (Yellow–Orange) for detailed session notes.

Reading check

- Before reading, check that children know the meaning of less familiar words:

  ### Jump On!
  zip – to run fast
  snap – to take a photo

  ### The Big Bug
  vast – enormous

- During reading, check that children can recall the GPCs j, v, w, z, zz and use this knowledge to blend and read words in the story, e.g. jump, visit, well, zip, buzz.

New to CODE?
Don't forget to read the launch story and watch the animation at
www.oxfordprimary.co.uk

Oxford OWL

For school
Discover eBooks, inspirational resources, advice and support

For home
Helping your child's learning with free eBooks, essential tips and fun activities

www.oxfordowl.co.uk